Vince Carter

Slam Dunk Artist

Vince Carter

Slam Dunk Artist

John Albert Torres

Enslow Publishers, Inc.

40 Industrial Road   PO Box 38
Box 398   Aldershot
Berkeley Heights, NJ 07922   Hants GU12 6BP
USA   UK

http://www.enslow.com

Library of Congress Cataloging-in-Publication Data

Torres, John Albert.
    Vince Carter : slam dunk artist / John Albert Torres.
        v. cm. — (Sports leaders series)
    Includes bibliographical references and index.
    Contents: Greatest game—Growing up—The big recruit—Tar heel super-
star—The NBA—A genuine good guy.
    ISBN 0-7660-2173-4
        1. Carter, Vince—Juvenile literature. 2. Basketball players—United States—
Biography—Juvenile literature. [1. Carter, Vince. 2. Basketball players.
3. African Americans—Biography.] I. Title. II. Series.
GV884.C39T67   2004
796.323'092—dc22

                                                            2003027974

Printed in the United States of America

10 9 8 7 6 5 4 3 2

To Our Readers: We have done our best to make sure all Internet Addresses in this book were active and appropriate when we went to press. However, the author and the publisher have no control over and assume no liability for the material available on those Internet sites or on other Web sites they may link to. Any comments or suggestions can be sent by e-mail to comments@enslow.com or to the address on the back cover.

Illustration Credits: Al Bello/Getty Images, p. 34; Barry Gossage/NBAE/ Getty Images, pp. 10, 14, 16, 18; Brian Bahr/Getty Images, p. 54; Craig Jones/Getty Images, pp. 44, 51, 57; Doug Pensinger/Getty Images, pp. 46, 60; Ezra O. Shaw/Allsport, p. 80; Fernando Medina/NBAE/Getty Images, p. 38; Garrett Ellwood/NBAE/Getty Images, p. 69; Jed Jacobsohn/Allsport, p. 71; Jed Jacobsohn/Getty Images, pp. 6, 32, 42, 66; Lisa Blumenfeld/Getty Images, p. 31; Otto Greule Jr./ALLSPORT, p. 28; Robert Laberge/Allsport, pp. 20, 62, 74; Robert Skeoch/Allsport, p. 76; Robert Skeoch/Getty Images, p. 40; Ron Turenne/NBAE via Getty Images, pp. 24, 84, 88, 92.

Cover Illustration: Jed Jacobsohn/Getty Images.

CONTENTS

GREATEST GAME

It was a television moment that nearly every basketball fan will remember. The date was February 13, 2000, the day of the annual NBA All-Star game.

A timeout was called on the floor and the network broke to a commercial. That is when Vince Carter, the All-Star nicknamed "Showtime" and "Air Canada," faced the fiercest competition any NBA player ever has and probably ever will.

No, the Toronto Raptor superstar was not facing off against Michael Jordan, Allen Iverson, or Kobe Bryant. Instead, the smiling master of the slam dunk went one-on-one against a fierce velociraptor dinosaur during a sports-drink commercial. The spot ends with Carter on his back after the dinosaur has slam dunked the ball, saying he thinks he needs more of the sports drink.

The raptor versus Raptor commercial became a favorite among basketball and Vince Carter fans for years to come. And the concept was not so far-fetched. The scoring machine has had some tough battles during his NBA career. Some have even put him on the injured list.

Because of Carter's injuries, some people have labeled him as being a "soft" player. This means that a player is afraid of physical contact and is content with simply shooting jump shots and not going after rebounds. But those players closest to Carter know he has the heart of a lion.

"Anybody who thinks he's soft, they don't understand basketball," said former teammate Hakeem Olajuwon. "A soft player does not have that energy, that aggressiveness. He gets beat up a lot. Teams attack him every night. How can he be soft?"[1]

That rough play is actually a strategy that some teams are trying out on the league's premiere dunker and finisher at the rim. But what caused some teams to start treating Carter roughly on the basketball court is that they found him to be nearly impossible to defend.

Right from the start of his professional basketball career Carter has proven that he is a scoring machine. Carter is one of those rare players who combines explosive speed with pure grace. He is one of those players who is beautiful to watch. Another thing that quickly made him a fan favorite early in his career was that big grin. Carter was one of the few great basketball players who did not seem angry at the world. He smiled, he laughed, he shook hands with referees and opposing players. Sometimes Carter just looked like a big kid out there on the court having fun.

> "Anybody who thinks he's soft, they don't understand basketball."
>
> —Hakeem Olajuwon, on Vince Carter

Carter will also spend hours after ballgames or practices signing autographs for the kids. He loved watching his favorite players as a child, and he knows that the experience of attending a basketball game is a special moment.

Sometimes, though, Carter's smile gets him in trouble with the referees. He wears a lot of expressions on his face, and sometimes the officials think he is arguing a call or making fun of the other team.

Vince Carter shoots over the outstretched arm of Bo Outlaw of the Phoenix Suns.

But in reality, Carter is just smiling and having a good time.

"He's just trying to get the crowd riled up and they take it as embarrassing," said teammate Tracy Murray about the referees.[2]

Former teammate Charles Oakley said that sometimes Carter is too nice for his own good.

"He wants to be friends with everybody," said the player known as the Oak Man. "You are one of the best players in the league, you don't need friends. Friends will come."[3]

So will the points. Lots of them. From the moment he first put on a Raptors uniform, Carter became very comfortable scoring points in bunches.

But not many NBA players can boast of ever having a night like Carter did on February 27, 2000, when he was in just his second season. That night Carter scored 51 points in an incredible performance against the Phoenix Suns. Better yet, the game was nationally televised on NBC, so all of America got to watch the young superstar in action.

In fact, NBC changed its schedule around so that it could show the Raptors game. This was only two weeks after Carter had won the slam-dunk contest at the All-Star game, graced the cover of *Sports Illustrated* magazine, and faced off against the terrifying dinosaur in the sports-drink commercial. Now, just about everyone who knew anything about basketball knew who Vince Carter was.

And the Raptors needed just about every one of the points he scored to come away with the 103–102 victory.

Carter knew he was off to a good start early in the game when his jump shot was falling and his drives to the basket seemed effortless. During one stretch, late in the second quarter, Carter hit back-to-back three-pointers, and then followed that up with a thunderous two-handed slam dunk that brought the crowd to its feet and gave the Raptors a nine-point lead. Carter went into the locker room waving to the crowd and giving high-fives to fans along the way. Once again Vince Carter was having fun playing a kid's game.

> From the moment he first put on a Raptors uniform, Carter became very comfortable scoring points in bunches.

The halftime break did not slow him down at all. Just a few minutes into the third quarter, Carter showed great body control by executing a spinning 360-degree layup that drew a foul from Anfernee Hardaway. NBC replayed the highlight over and over again. Carter spun his entire body around while in mid-air, and still knew exactly where the basket was in order to put the ball through. Then, a few seconds after sinking the free throw, Carter threw down an alley-oop dunk on a pass from teammate Tracy McGrady. The crowd went wild. Phoenix was doing a good job at keeping the game close, and Carter's slam dunk gave the Raptors a 62–57 lead.

The teams see-sawed for the rest of the contest, keeping fans at the edge of their seats. Then with 47 seconds left, Carter had the ball with the Raptors clinging to a 101–99 lead. The Suns were now double-teaming him. This meant that they had two players guarding the game's top scorer. But it had little effect on Carter.

He dribbled at the top of the key, then faked to his right before starting a drive toward the basket by going left. At first Carter was looking to pass to an open man. But his quickness allowed him to explode past the two defenders and suddenly he had a clear path to the basket. Carter's eyes lit up. He moved the ball from his left hand to his right and scooped in a picture-perfect layup. The sellout crowd stood and cheered. The arena seemed to be rocking on its foundations.

When he ran down the court, Carter could not

Carter is guarded by the Suns' Dan Majerle as he dribbles the ball near midcourt at America West Arena in Phoenix, Arizona.

help but look over in the stands at his mother. He knew that he had just scored his 51st point of the game! Carter knew the magnitude, or importance, of what he had just done. In a country known more for its great hockey teams and the cold weather, Carter had single-handedly put basketball on the map in Canada. His slam-dunk performance, and now this, would cause thousands of youngsters to ask their parents for Vince Carter jerseys. Basketball had arrived in Canada, and its name was Vince Carter.

"I didn't want to show it, but inside I was like a little kid," Carter said after the game. "I looked over at my mom and thought she was going to flip out of her seat."[4]

But even after scoring his 51st point, the game was still in jeopardy because Rodney Rogers of the Suns raced downcourt and nailed a three-pointer to make it a one-point game with 37 ticks left on the clock.

Then, the Raptors could not get a good shot at the basket and lost the ball to the Suns on a shot clock violation. But Raptor forward Charles Oakley got his hand on the ball as Rogers was driving toward the basket and knocked it away as time

Vince Carter skies for a rebound during a game against the Suns in Phoenix.

expired. Carter and the Raptors had held on for the victory.

Carter was ecstatic after the game and as usual tried to give a lot of the credit for his scoring barrage to his teammates. He kept saying it was a team effort and that the most important thing was not the number of points he scored but that the team won such a hard-fought battle.

"It feels good to get 51 but it hasn't sunk in yet," a smiling Carter told reporters after the game. "I wanted the ball in my hands where I could make a decision. I was hitting shots, but if I wasn't I wanted to get the double team and find the open man. Everything else is going to go unnoticed today because of the 51 points [but] we did it all as a team today."[5]

In all, Carter made 17 of 32 field goal attempts and was 13 for 13 from the foul line. He had 4 three-pointers, pulled down 9 rebounds, and had 3 steals.

Even Carter's coach, Butch Carter, was amazed.

"The young legend grows," the coach said. "No one's more surprised today than me."[6]

If Carter's coach knew anything about the type of childhood that Vince Carter had, the kind of love and support he was surrounded with, then he

Carter throws a long pass upcourt to an open teammate during a fast break.

would have known that Carter could probably do anything—if he sets his mind to it.

Yes, Vince Carter had a childhood unlike many of the other NBA superstars who came before him. The result, however, has proven to be the same: Vince Carter is an NBA great.

GROWING UP

Vincent Lamar Carter was born on January 26, 1977. Vince grew up without his biological father playing a role in his life. In fact, to this day, he has never played a part in Vince's life. Fortunately for Vince, his mother, Michelle Carter-Robinson, was a well-grounded career woman and was able to provide him with a solid foundation of support during his childhood. Because his mother had a good job as a teacher, she was also able to raise Vince in a nice, upper-middle class neighborhood in Daytona Beach, Florida.

When he was seven years old, Vince's life became even more solidified when his mother married Harry

Robinson. Seeing him as more than just a stepfather, Vince called Robinson "Dad." Like Vince's mom, Robinson was also a teacher. He recently retired after spending almost forty years in the education field. Naturally, one can imagine how much education was stressed in the Carter household.

"Vince is a very fortunate young man," said Carter's mother, Michelle. "In the United States there are a great number of children who are raised in single-parent homes. Having two parents makes a huge difference to kids in terms of guidance and dealing with social problems."[1]

Besides education, the other thing that was stressed in Vince's house while growing up was discipline. His mother sometimes treated Vince like the thousands of students that she taught. She did not cut her son any slack. This was evident in Vince's good grades and the good behavior he exhibited while in school. Vince never failed a class and never got into trouble. Even as a child, he was a role model for other children to follow.

> "Having two parents makes a huge difference to kids in terms of guidance and dealing with social problems."
>
> —Michelle Carter-Robinson

"He was never treated as special," said Charles Brinkerhoff, Vince's basketball coach later on in high school. "His mom was always good at keeping outside influences away. He was never treated any different than any other kid."[2]

From a young age, Vince loved sports and showed everyone how good he was.

His favorite, right from the start, was basketball. Vince was always tall for his age, and that helped, but he was also very athletic and naturally graceful. A basketball in his hand seemed like a natural fit.

One of the main reasons Vince loved basketball so much had to do with his uncle, Oliver Lee, a former college basketball star who then went on for a short stint in the NBA with the Chicago Bulls. Lee, who led the Marquette University basketball team in scoring, spent a lot of time with young Vince, showing him the finer points of the game.

Even today, Carter credits his uncle with taking him under his wing and properly teaching him the game of basketball. Little did Lee know at the time that his pupil would one day become an NBA superstar.

Vince loved basketball so much as a child that whenever he would go shopping with his mother, he refused to walk with her. Instead, he needed room to pretend he was dribbling a basketball. He would

Vince Carter smiles during pregame introductions prior to a game against the Pistons in Toronto, Canada, on April 1, 2003.

imitate moves he had seen on television, driving to imaginary baskets in his mind.

Later on in his NBA career, Vince Carter would often be compared to the legendary Michael Jordan. It is a natural association, since both players are known for their high-flying moves on the court. But even before Vince Carter's basketball talents began to blossom, he knew he wanted to "be like Mike" (as the old television commercials used to say). As early as the seventh grade, Vince wanted to wear Jordan's No. 23 for his junior high school team. "But he knew he probably wouldn't get it," his mother, Michelle Carter-Robinson, remembered. "I told him, 'It would make us so proud if you picked a different number and made that one famous.' So he chose 15 and the rest is history. I've always tried to instill in him not to be a follower, to make your own path."[3]

This is exactly what Vince did. He chose No. 15 and would stick with it through high school, college, and the pros. Today, Carter's No. 15 is nearly as recognizable as Jordan's No. 23. The number is significant. "One plus five is six," Michelle Carter-Robinson explained. "The Roman numeral for six is VI. I didn't know the number's significance until I discovered people calling him VI, short for Vince."[4]

Vince had another love, in addition to basketball.

He also loved music. Vince's mother always made sure that Vince knew there was a lot more to life than just dribbling a basketball.

"As a teacher, I knew the value of exposing him to a lot of different things," said his mother, Michelle Carter-Robinson. "We kept him very active. I guess that's why he turned out to be such a good kid. We kept him busy and he didn't have time to get into any trouble."[5]

While his mother gets the credit for making sure Vince was well rounded, his love of music comes from his stepfather, Harry Robinson, who was a band leader and music teacher.

Vince would tinker around his stepfather's music room and play with the instruments. He would finger the keyboards and blow on the horns. His favorite, though, was always the saxophone.

When Vince was old enough to go to high school, he transferred out of his district to a different school. He did not do this because he wanted to play on a better basketball team, but so he could play music in his stepfather's band—one of the best in the country.

At Mainland High School, Vince played the baritone saxophone and then was even the drum major. The drum major position is usually reserved for a true leader. It is the one person who ensures that all the marchers are in unison and that everyone stays in rhythm.

"I love music and I loved being the drum major," Vince said. "As the drum major, there's a lot of conducting, arranging and organizing. It was probably the toughest job at our school, besides principal.

"I knew a lot of people laughed at that job," Carter continued, "But it's more leadership than any of them realized. I had to keep a whole bunch of people together at practices—that's where I did the most work, at practice. I had to keep them quiet, keep them in line. It was hard to explain to people who only watched us march on the football field."[6]

> "I've always tried to instill in him not to be a follower, to make your own path."
> —Michelle Carter-Robinson

"His junior year he played the baritone saxophone," Michelle Carter-Robinson recalled, "but then his senior year he was the drum major. He's tall and thin, so anything he put on looked good on him. He had on one of those tall white hats that made him look even taller, and a white uniform with gold buttons. He just looked terrific."[7]

Vince was not just flashy in his white drum

Carter goes up for a dunk during a game against the Seattle Supersonics at the Key Arena in Seattle on March 9, 2001.

major uniform. He was also flashy in the school's home white basketball uniforms, where he started "posterizing" kids from rival schools on a regular basis with his intense slam dunks and high-flying acrobatics.

The fans began calling him UFO, because he always seemed to be flying in the air. They would sometimes even chant it during games.

Although Vince was blessed with incredible athleticism and talent, it was not raw talent alone that set him apart from the other boys his age. Quite simply, Vince was the hardest worker on his team.

"His work ethic is what really separated him from the other top players in America," said his high school basketball coach Charlie Brinkerhoff. "I'm not saying the others didn't work hard, but Vince was always the first player in the gym and always the last one to leave. I almost had to pry the ball out of his hands and tell him to get out."[8]

One example of working hard at his game occurred during the summer of 1992. While his friends were hanging out at nearby world-famous Daytona Beach, Vince decided that it was time to learn something new to add to his already great basketball skills.

He worked every day of the summer teaching

himself to shoot a basketball left-handed. He got so good at it that Vince even learned how to eat with his left hand and throw a football as well. The new skills came in handy over the years when Vince hurt his right wrist a few times playing basketball. In fact, the following summer he scored a whopping 34 points left-handed—including 5 three-pointers—at a team camp practice game at Florida State University.

A year later, Vince re-injured his wrist at the Beach Ball Classic Tournament. During the game, Vince had to switch and play left-handed. He hit 4 of 8 free throws, blocked a shot, and even threw down a left-handed slam dunk.

During the summer between sophomore and junior seasons, Vince attended some national basketball tournaments. That is when Vince's confidence really started to grow. That is when he learned that he could play with older, stronger, and better players. He attended the Nike camp and the Five Star camp, where he played against future NBA stars like Kevin Garnett and Ron Mercer.

"They were bigger and stronger than Vince," said his basketball coach, Brinkerhoff. "But even then you could see he had so much athleticism."[9]

Although he was clearly the team's superstar, even in high school Vince was the ultimate team

Carter looks on from the bench during a game against the Clippers in Los Angeles in 2003.

Carter goes for the windmill dunk. Carter began to gain a reputation as a slam-dunk artist while still in high school.

player. As a junior he had to play out of position, moving from guard to forward. He averaged 25 points per game and grabbed 11 rebounds per contest while leading the team to a 30–2 record. Brinkerhoff said that having Vince on the team was like having another coach on the floor.

If Brinkerhoff and Vince thought the attention and excitement were there during Vince's junior year, they would be in for quite a surprise during Vince's astonishing senior year—one in which just about every major college wanted Vince to come play for them.

THE BIG RECRUIT

By the end of his junior year, Vince Carter had established himself as a great high school basketball player. But it was in the state playoffs that those outside of Volusia County began taking notice.

Vince's Mainland High School team was set to face a powerful Jacksonville Mandarin team that was heavily favored. The winning team would advance further into the state playoffs; the losers would be going home.

Right before the game—played in front of a packed gymnasium—Coach Brinkerhoff took Vince aside to let him know how important the game was. The coach told him to keep playing unselfishly, but he also told Vince that he had the ability to take the game over if he wanted to.

This is exactly what Vince Carter did.

Vince scored an astonishing 47 points and grabbed 13 rebounds, leading the team to a hard-fought victory. His scoring showcased just what a talented and versatile player Vince was even in high school. He scored 18 of his points from behind the three-point line, and he had 14 points on dunks!

After the game, even Vince was amazed.

"I had 35 points in the first half," he recalled. "It was a situation where I felt like I was ball-hogging, but Coach Brinkerhoff said to take every good, open shot I got. And the shot was falling."[1]

To this day, Coach Brinkerhoff cannot help but to smile when he talks about that game.

"That was the most incredible offensive game I've seen him have," he said. "He could have done that a lot of other times but he's extremely unselfish. It was a game I didn't want him to be unselfish. I wanted him to show the others how to play at that level."[2]

By the time he was a senior, college scouts were at his regular games and even stayed to watch him work out. The recruiting full-court press was on.

But Vince did not let anything distract him. Right

from the start of the season, Vince's presence on the court made him a force to be reckoned with. The human UFO made a habit of scoring tons of points and walking off the court a winner.

He averaged 22 points, 11.4 rebounds, 4.5 assists, and 3.5 blocks per game. In one game, Vince scored 26 points, pulled down 16 rebounds, dished out 8 assists, and blocked 17 shots—showing that he could also play a bit of defense!

It came as a surprise to no one that Carter received 29 of 33 first-place votes to be named Florida's "Mr. Basketball." That is what his friends started calling him.

Even before Vince Carter had committed to a college, he had begun to draw interest from some NBA teams. One of those teams was the Toronto Raptors, who were not in the habit of scouting high school players, but even they had heard of the "UFO." Bob Zuffelato, who worked for the Raptors, received a phone call from an old friend who happened to be the athletic director at Mainland. His friend, Dick

> "That was the most incredible offensive game I've seen him have. He could have done that a lot of other times but he's extremely unselfish."
>
> —Coach Brinkerhoff

Vince Carter sails high above the rim just before he is about to make another highlight-reel dunk.

Toth, could not stop raving about a kid named Vince Carter.

But Vince would not go the way of Kevin Garnett and skip college to go right to the pros. He wanted an education to fall back on just in case his basketball career fizzled. Vince was recruited by schools all over the country, but he quickly narrowed his choice down to four schools. He was interested in playing for and attending basketball powerhouses Duke or North Carolina. But he was also giving serious consideration to the University of Florida and Florida State—two schools more known for their football programs—because they were close to home.

The head coach for the University of Florida Gators, Lon Kruger, made things tough for Vince because he was the only coach to watch Vince play the NCAA-maximum four times each season. He also became close friends with Vince and his mother. Kruger really wanted Vince to become a Gator. Vince was very close to choosing the University of Florida. In fact, he was one of 10,000 fans who poured into UF's gymnasium for "Midnight Madness" on October 15, 1994. Midnight madness is the first time a college team can practice together for the season. Many schools hold a pep rally and first practice on midnight of the first eligible day of practice.

Carter clamps down defensively against David Wesley of the Charlotte Hornets during a game at the Air Canada Center in Toronto in November 2000.

That was during a time when the University of Florida basketball program was considered very strong and the team actually made it to the coveted NCAA Final Four. But then the Gators fell on hard times and even lost several games to lowly schools, including Jacksonville that December. Vince was afraid that FSU, or the Seminoles, would go the same route, so he narrowed his choices to North Carolina or Duke.

Coaches from both schools were salivating at the thought of having Vince Carter—who had 92 slam dunks in 36 games as a high school senior—play for their team. Carter had proven himself a scoring machine throughout high school. He led Mainland in scoring for his sophomore, junior, and senior seasons, with 506, 813, and 720 points, respectively.

Now, at the same time, it was not just basketball coaches who were offering Vince a chance at a free education. Vince also received several musical scholarships from major universities. But Vince's first love was basketball.

According to his high school coach, Brinkerhoff, the deciding factor for Vince was that he wanted a chance to go to a school that was diverse and offered wide varieties in fields of study. Daytona Beach in

Carter slams home another dunk. After high school, Carter brought his high-flying game to the University of North Carolina.

Florida is a diverse area, and Vince Carter wanted to maintain that feeling.

"Vince said we needed to learn that it's more important to accept people for whatever they are; that it doesn't mean we have to become what they are," the coach said. "In high school, he [Vince] got along with all kinds of people."[3]

Brinkerhoff, and many others, credit Vince's mother with raising such a special person, who also turned out to be a one-in-a-million basketball talent.

"There's nobody on the planet who is as good a guardian as his mom," Brinkerhoff said.[4]

But Vince's stepfather, Harry Robinson, said that Vince should receive most of the credit for how he turned out.

"People always try to give me and his mother credit as good parents, but Vince would have turned out to be a good person no matter who his parents were," Robinson said.[5]

The desire for a well-rounded education and inspiration from legendary coach Dean Smith were the deciding factors for Vince. He would follow in the footsteps of number 23, Michael Jordan, and go to the University of North Carolina. Vince Carter was going to be a Tar Heel!

Carter was impressed with Coach Smith right

Head Coach Dean Smith, Assistant Coach Bill Guthridge, and Vince Carter (left to right) confer during a timeout. The presence of Coach Smith was a big factor in Carter's decision to attend UNC.

from the start. In fact, Carter remembers that during one of his first conversations with Smith, basketball was not even among the first things discussed. Instead, Smith chose to first talk about the great academic support at the college, the wonderful faculty and staff, and the wonderful opportunities for college life at the university at Chapel Hill.

"This went on for at least an hour," Carter recalled. "He had me really confused." Smith did not tell him how badly he wanted him to play at UNC or what a great player he was. He simply told him that

UNC was a place of great opportunities. "I really didn't understand any of it until I realized that's just Coach Smith. That's the way he is. He really had me confused. About an hour later, he started talking about basketball."[6]

Vince Carter would have a lot of big names to live up to as he packed his belongings to head off to college. There was, of course, Michael Jordan. But UNC had produced a number of superstar NBA players over the years, including James Worthy and Sam Perkins.

Would Carter be able to live up to the hype? Would he lead UNC to the Final Four? Would he make the NBA?

The pressure was on right from the start. Carter attended a college football game at the school and some students told Carter he was a basketball god and that he would lead UNC to a title.

TAR HEEL SUPERSTAR

Vince Carter received no promises form the University of North Carolina coaching staff about playing time or anything else. All they told the kid from Daytona Beach, Florida, was that if he worked hard and followed the program, then he had a chance to do some great things in the world of college basketball.

Carter was impressed right from the start.

"After my first week of practice with him [Coach Smith], I just sat home and thought about how much basketball I had learned. I was a totally different player. Young players think they know everything about basketball. Coach Smith just starts you over [and] shows you how much you didn't know."[1]

While Carter did carry a lot of pressure with him because he was such a heralded high school player, he was not the only freshman on the basketball team. The Tar Heels were lucky enough to recruit Antawn Jamison from Charlotte, North Carolina, as well. Jamison was also an All-American high school basketball player and was heavily recruited by the major colleges. Another freshman, Ademola Okulaja was also recruited. The three young players quickly formed a bond at practice and on and off the court. They became nearly inseparable as they compared basketball notes and class notes, trying to succeed. They became know to their friends as the "Three Musketeers."

But Carter, who had come from a free and open offensive-minded basketball system in high school, had a hard time adjusting to college basketball. One thing that Coach Smith did not like to do was give his freshman too much playing time. More than a decade earlier, Smith had even written a newspaper article for *The New York Times* titled "Why Freshmen Should Not Play." Smith believed that the freshmen should sit and learn while upperclassmen played the majority of minutes on the court. Coach Smith also stressed tough defense and multiple substitutions to get everyone a lot of playing time and keep bodies fresh.

Despite this, Coach Smith found that his "Three Musketeers" were just too good to keep on the bench. By the time the Atlantic Coast Conference (ACC) games began, Carter was starting at guard, while Jamison and Okulaja started as the forwards. In the season opener against North Carolina State before a sold-out crowd of 21,572 at the Dean Dome, Carter scored a season-high 18 points to lead the Tar Heels to a 96–72 victory.

> **"Young players think they know everything about basketball. Coach Smith just starts you over [and] shows you how much you didn't know."**
>
> **—Vince Carter**

As the season progressed, however, Carter quickly saw his playing time cut as he could not grasp the team's defensive oriented style of play. Meanwhile, his friends, Jamison and Okulaja, were playing often and well. Carter became worried that he would not be able to succeed at this level. In fact, lots of people were worried. Lots of people, except for Coach Dean Smith.

"I was concerned that he had unrealistic expectations, which most young, highly recruited players have," Smith said. "I thought he was progressing at an excellent pace, but everyone else said 'What's wrong with Carter?' Well, that meant their expectations were unrealistic and uninformed."[2]

Carter had never been a part-time player before in his life. As a player who leaves a lot of his emotion out there for everyone to see, the transformation from superstar to role player was very hard for Carter to take at first.

Still, Carter wound up scoring in double figures in ten games, including 14 points against an eighth-ranked Wake Forest that was led by a young Tim Duncan. In the game, Carter had five second-half baskets, including a spectacular reverse layup that cut Wake Forest's lead to two. He capped the game with a soaring alley-oop slam as the Tar Heels won, 65–59. Carolina played well enough to make the NCAA Tournament, but they bowed out early in a second-round loss to Texas Tech.

As a rookie, Carter averaged only 7.5 points and 3.8 rebounds per game. But he decided that he would make himself ready for whatever the team needed.

"I kind of wanted to go out there and just figure it out myself and just play harder," Carter said. "I was asked to play a few minutes, but I accepted that, and that's what made me—I think—a bigger man."[3]

Vince Carter looks to pass during the Pepsi Challenge game on December 7, 1996. The UNC Tarheels defeated the South Carolina Gamecocks in the game, 86–75.

Like he had done once before in high school, Carter decided to spend his summer vacation working on his basketball skills. He was disappointed after his freshman campaign but decided not to feel sad about it. Instead, he went to work.

Carter made it a habit to start every day of the summer shooting 500 times from all over the basketball court. Then he would play pickup games with older and tougher players to try and work on his defense and passing ability. Carter knew that he could probably score on just about anybody, but he needed to work on the weaker parts of his game if he was going to help out his college team.

He also decided that for his sophomore season, he would work hard all the time, regardless of the playing time he received.

"I wanted to be a plus and not a minus for this team," he said. "I wasn't really dedicating myself to the team the way I should have. I wasn't playing as hard as I could. I don't think I was giving it 100 percent every night."[4]

It takes a big man to realize when he needs to step it up and work harder.

Carter's hard work paid immediate dividends for his team. He averaged nearly 14 points and 5 rebounds per game for the season's first 10 games as the Tar Heels ran up a 9–1 record. But Carter suffered a minor injury and the Tar Heels lost their next three games to Wake Forest, Maryland, and Virginia. Carter and his teammates would avenge these losses once his bruised hip was fully recovered.

On February 20, Carter was deadly accurate from the field. He made 9 out of 10 shots to tally a career-high 26 points and lead the twelfth-ranked Tar Heels to an easy victory against the fourth-ranked Wake Forest Demon Deacons with Tim Duncan. Early in the first half of the game, Carter brought down the house when he caught an alley-oop pass from teammate Ed Cota to throw down a thunderous slam dunk. That play sparked a 14–2 Tar Heel run that made the score 26–11 for North Carolina. The Tar Heels never looked back.

> "I wanted to be a plus and not a minus for this team."
> —Vince Carter

What really made Carter happy was that Coach Smith praised Carter's defensive play, calling him a complete player.

Carter and his teammates rolled from that point onward and easily qualified for the NCAA "March Madness" tournament. In the tournament, the Tar Heels reached the Sweet 16 by defeating Fairfield

Carter brings the ball upcourt during the Tarheels' Final Four game against the Arizona Wildcats on March 29, 1997.

and Colorado. In the round of 16, the Heels found themselves in a tight contest with California. With the score tied at 48 late in the game, Carter took over. He slammed home a dunk to put the Tar Heels up by two. Then, after a Cal miss, he pushed the ball quickly downcourt, pulled up and hit a clutch three-pointer. Carolina went on to win, 63–57, and entered the round of 8.

Before a packed house against Louisville, Vince Carter scored 13 points in the first half to lead the Tar Heels to an early 21-point advantage in the game. But the Cardinals fought back, eventually narrowing the Tar Heels' lead to just three points. This is when Vince Carter stepped up to make the biggest bucket of his team's season. He took the ball downcourt, shook past three defenders and hit a running lay-up. Everyone in the building could feel the game turn on the play. The Tar Heels went on to win easily by a final score of 97–74.

The team had rolled through four wins in the tournament, sixteen straight victories overall, and were set to face the tough Arizona Wildcats in the Final Four. There was one stretch early in the game in which Arizona simply was not quick enough to catch Carter in transition. Carter would release when a shot was put up and simply outrun the opposing team to catch an outlet pass downcourt. At one point, he scored an amazing 13 points in a row! By halftime some Arizona players said it felt as if Carter dunked on them 12 times in a row. But Arizona's stifling defense clamped down on Carter and his teammates in the second half and pulled out the victory, 66–58. Arizona went on to win the national title.

Both Carter and his buddy Jamison were back for their junior seasons at UNC, and they were determined to lead the team back to another Final Four appearance. Preseason rankings gave the team the number 4 ranking in the country. The Tar Heels began the season against seventh-ranked UCLA, and the contest was not even close. Carter scored 22 points from the small forward position to lead the Tar Heels to a 109–68 rout.

Carter had a great season as he continued to concentrate on being more of a team player and not looking for his shot as much as he could. The result? Carter led the Atlantic Coast Conference with an incredible .591 shooting percentage. This meant that Carter made nearly 6 out of every 10 shots he took! He averaged 15.6 points and 5.1 boards per game to be named First Team All-Atlantic Coast Conference and Second Team All-American.

Carter and his UNC teammates celebrate on the sidelines during a playoff game in March 1997.

Carter made so many thrilling slam dunks and incredible under-pressure shots as a junior that the comparisons to Michael Jordan started being heard everywhere. Professional scouts were now regulars at all of North Carolina's games as they started scouting Carter and Jamison together. Jamison had announced that he would leave school after his junior season to become a professional, but Carter had yet to declare anything. One thing was certain: The NBA was ready for Vince Carter.

> Carter had a great season as he continued to concentrate on being more of a team player and not looking for his shot as much as he could.

In one game during the NCAA tournament, Carter scored 17 of his season-high 24 points in the second half and in overtime, helping the Tar Heels edge rival UNC-Charlotte. In the game, Carter also had 7 rebounds, passed for a couple of assists, and blocked a big shot in overtime. Incredibly, he played 42 minutes that game without turning the ball over once!

This was easily the best game of Carter's college career. Carter kept his team close in the first half, but the Tar Heels found themselves behind 36–32 at halftime. Carter spoke to his teammates at halftime about intensity and playing hard. It worked.

Carter took a pass to begin the second half and drained a three-pointer that sparked a run of 12 unanswered points. But UNC-Charlotte would not go away. The 49ers battled back to 47–44 by playing good defense and executing patient offense. That is when Carter took over once again. He scored his team's next eight points to restore their comfortable lead. But once again the 49ers did not give up. They tied the score and forced overtime.

This is when Carter stunned the crowd with the play of the game. The Tar Heels were holding onto a two-point lead with just under two minutes left in overtime when Charlotte's Sean Colson seemed to have a wide-open short jump shot lined up. But Carter streaked down the court and seemed to come from nowhere. He blocked the shot, stripped Colson of the loose ball, and then fired a rocket of a pass to teammate Shammond Williams, who was fouled. Williams made both free throws and the Tar Heels pulled away with the victory.

Then, in the Eastern regional final of the NCAA tournament, Carter's mission was to stop the University of Connecticut's Richard Hamilton from scoring. The Big East Player of the Year was a scoring machine, and Carter relished the challenge of trying to stop him. Carter used his newfound defensive

Carter hoists the ACC tournament trophy after UNC defeated North Carolina State to take the title on March 9, 1997.

skills as well as pure athleticism to hold Hamilton to 5 of 21 from the field.

"It was an opportunity for me to go against a great offensive player and I accept challenges like that," Carter said after the game. "It was a tough task from start to finish but I thought it was going to be a tough task for him, too."[5]

The Tar Heels defeated UConn to make it to their second consecutive Final Four appearance. Unfortunately, Carter was the only player who seemed to bring his "A" game. He scored a team-high 21 points on 10 of 16 shooting, but the Tar Heels were defeated by Utah. But making the Final Four two years running is still a great accomplishment. Some teams go years and years without making it to the Final Four.

After the season, Carter would be faced with a serious decision. Would he stay for a senior year at UNC or would he try his luck in the NBA?

THE NBA

Carter had a lot of things to think about. He was enjoying his team at UNC and had become one of the best college basketball players in the country. He had already led his team to two Final Four appearances, but now with Antawn Jamison going to the NBA, Carter knew the team would have to rebuild a bit.

Finally, Carter thought about himself and his family. Then the decision came easily. Carter was giving up the final year at UNC to play professionally in the NBA.

"The team had a great time, we're all very close, and we played well together on the floor, but sometimes you have to be selfish and say, 'what's good for Vince?'" he said. "I talked to my teammates and they were all behind me, so it made it easier."[1]

This is when things got funny and forever linked Vince Carter and Antawn Jamison. The two teammates had become very close friends at UNC, and Carter even spent long weekends at Jamison's family home in Charlotte. Both players were projected to go in the NBA lottery and both were expected to be top-10 picks.

> "The team had a great time, we're all very close, and we played well together on the floor."
>
> —Vince Carter

The Golden State Warriors had the fifth pick in the draft, and they really wanted Jamison. But they heard that the Dallas Mavericks were also interested in Jamison. The Mavericks were talking about switching picks with the Toronto Raptors, who had the fourth pick in the draft. So Golden State offered Toronto $250,000 to take Jamison and then trade him for Vince Carter, whom they would take with the next pick.

That is exactly what happened. The two college teammates went fourth and fifth in the draft, and then were immediately traded for each other. Carter was now a Toronto Raptor, and fans in Canada could not have been happier.

Raptors general manager Glen Grunwald had his eye on Carter right from the start. "I just felt Vince was more versatile [than Jamison]," he said. "He had better athleticism and overall skills. He had not been known as an outside shooter, but there was no reason he couldn't develop into a good outside shooter."[2]

North Carolina proved to be a good training ground for Carter, who, like Michael Jordan before him, blossomed when he made it to the NBA. He no longer had to worry about strict offensive sets or teams playing a stifling zone defense against him. Carter now was able to open things up and play his game. Carter immediately started dazzling fans and media alike with his wide array of slam dunks and high-flying acrobatics.

Canada fell in love with Carter immediately, and he is credited with saving a franchise that had been in trouble. People flocked to the games to see the rookie play. They hounded him for autographs and followed him wherever he went. Carter loved every minute of it. He would stop for hours and talk to the fans, signing autographs for everyone. Of course, his hard work ethic and good personality helped make him a fan favorite.

"I want to play hard for the fans," he said.

Vince Carter and college teammate Antawn Jamison (left to right) at the 1998 NBA Draft in June 1998.

"Sometimes I think they get a little too excited, but I think that's just the way it is. It's fun. I'm just glad that they enjoy it. I'm glad I can bring some excitement to the city."[3]

Carter brought lots of excitement to cities wherever the Raptors played. He averaged 18.3 points per game, 5.7 rebounds, and 3 assists to be the runaway choice for Rookie of the Year. After only one year, Carter seemed already to be on the verge of superstardom.

Meanwhile, Carter stayed close friends with Jamison, who was struggling mightily in Golden State, where he was relegated to the bench. Carter would call Jamison weekly to tell him to hang in there.

"I was just trying to encourage him and let him know [his] day would come," Carter said. "You don't want your friend only hearing what the doubters say. You want to pick him up and help him succeed. It's during times like that when you know who your real friends are."[4]

Carter's biggest fans, however, were not in Toronto, Canada. They were in Daytona Beach, Florida. Carter's family would gather at his parents' home and watch every game on satellite television. His mother would call him after the games and offer her advice. To this day, the two have a very close relationship.

Even though Carter was awarded the top rookie honor for his first season, his second season catapulted him into pure NBA superstardom. Carter set a team record by scoring 2,107 points and averaging 25.7 points per game—good enough for fourth best in the league. Carter led his team in scoring, field goal percentage, and percentage from behind the three-point arc. He was also second on the team in assists, third in blocks and steals, and fifth in rebounds.

Carter had become an NBA fan favorite and he was also starting to push the Raptors—a team known for bad records year after year—toward respectability. Carter won over so many fans that in just his second year of pro ball he was voted in as a starter for the 2000 All-Star game. Not only was he voted in, but he received the most votes of any player and the second highest amount ever with 1,911,973 votes. This was quite an accomplishment.

The day before the All-Star game, Carter wowed fans throughout the world with his incredible leaping ability and grace by winning the NBA Slam Dunk Contest. Past winners have included such NBA scoring legends as Michael Jordan and Dominique Wilkins. One of his winning dunks included Carter

Carter puts the ball through his legs in midair during one of his more spectacular dunks at the NBA All-Star Game Slam Dunk Contest at the Oakland Coliseum on February 12, 2000.

putting the ball through his legs while he seemed suspended in mid-air just below the rim. Then he took the ball with his right hand and slammed it through the basket.

But Carter's biggest accomplishment that season could not be measured in statistics. His great play and presence were enough to lead the Raptors to their first ever winning season and playoff berth. In just his second NBA season he had led his team to the playoffs! The team was eliminated in the first round, but it was certainly enough to cement Carter's superstar status.

While Carter was clearly at home on the basketball hardwood, he was still learning to adjust to life in Canada, where temperatures were nowhere near as warm as in Florida, where he had spent his whole life. Carter rented a luxury apartment on the shore of Lake Ontario near downtown Toronto.

Carter spent his first few years in Toronto staying close to his new home and getting to learn the city slowly.

"I don't go out much. I know enough to survive," he said. "I know where the grocery store is and where the arena is. I just really stay home, listen to music, play video games, and surf the Internet."[5]

Some of Carter's favorite video games include

Carter holds up the trophy he earned by winning the 2000 NBA
All-Star Game Slam Dunk Contest.

Madden Football and NBA Live. He also loves reading biographies, and his favorite one to read was the autobiography of civil rights activist Malcolm X.

That summer, after his second season, Carter was honored to be chosen to play for the United States Olympic team at the Olympics in Sydney, Australia. The team faced some stiff competition, especially from the European teams, but Carter was one of the main cogs in the gold-medal winning squad, leading the team in scoring with 14.8 points per game. During the games, Carter even got to dunk over a seven-foot-tall player!

Despite averaging more than 25 points per game and leading his team to the playoffs, Carter was nudged by coaches and basketball experts to look for his shot a little more often. That was the only way, they said, that he would be considered as one of the elite players like Shaquille O'Neal, Tim Duncan, Alan Iverson, and of course, Michael Jordan.

But Carter is a naturally unselfish person, and looking to shoot before passing is something he still has to get used to.

"I don't mind scoring the points that we need to win, but I don't mind passing the ball either," he said. "Every time I step on the court, I'm always looking to give the ball up, to get assists."[6]

Still, halfway through Carter's second season of professional basketball, there were some who said he should be considered the league's most valuable player for bringing the Raptors to respectability. Carter shied away from the MVP praise.

"I'm not the best player in the league. Not at all. Not yet," he said. "I have to just continue to get better. I figure I will be one of the best players in the league when I can help my team win consistently, night in and night out. Not sometimes. Not six in a row. But maybe 17, 18 in a row. I'm not saying I'm far behind, but I feel I can get better, and it's going to take a while. But I'm willing to learn, and I'm willing to wait my turn. I have to keep playing hard, keep learning, keep getting better and one day I could be the best player in the NBA."[7]

> "I don't mind scoring the points that we need to win. . . but I don't mind passing the ball either. . . . I'm always looking to give the ball up, to get assists."
>
> —Vince Carter

Once the Olympics were over, Carter returned to the United States and took a few weeks off from the daily basketball grind. There was something very important he needed to do. It was something that he promised his mother when he decided to leave college early and become an NBA

Living in Canada was an adjustment for Carter. He spent his first few years in Toronto staying close to home as he became more familiar with the city.

superstar. Carter was taking college classes in order to earn his degree in the field of African-American studies. Carter's mother would have it no other way.

"I made a promise that I would go back to school to finish my education," Carter said. "And that's what I intend to do."[8]

6

A
GENUINE
GOOD GUY

While Vince Carter started giving opposing coaches nightmares about how to contain such a potent scoring machine, fans, players, and media alike were starting to discover that in a league full of brash and arrogant players, Carter was a genuine good guy.

After just his second season, Carter received a $10,000 prize from the league for winning the NBA Sportsmanship Award. Carter was not excited about the money—he was excited about the prize. It was only natural, then, that Carter would donate the money to his old high school basketball team and marching band. It would not be the last time Carter would open up his wallet to help out Mainland High School.

On the court, new challenges awaited. With teams firmly intent on stopping Vince Carter and with the Raptors earning the respect of a bona fide NBA playoff team, it would certainly be difficult for Carter to top the 25.7 points per game he averaged in just his second season. But Carter found a way.

Using a combination of jump shots and attacks toward the basket, the man now known as "Air Canada" finished his third NBA season by averaging 27.6 points per game. Along with distant cousin and close friend Tracy McGrady, the duo formed one of the best one-two punches in the league.

Some people were comparing Carter and McGrady to the combination of Jordan and Pippen that helped the Chicago Bulls win so many championships during the 1990s. But what people fail to realize is that Michael Jordan was in the league a long time before he led his team to a title. In fact, Jordan was 28 and a five-time scoring champion in his seventh season by the time the Bulls won the NBA championship.

"The deeper the Bulls got in the playoffs, the greater was Michael's stature in the game," said Washington Wizards coach Doug Collins. "Vince

Carter has the talent. The next step will be his ability to take his team through the playoffs, like Bird, Magic, Isiah, Michael and now Kobe and Shaq."[1]

And even Carter shied away from the Michael Jordan comparisons. It's a lot of pressure to be compared to the man who many consider the greatest player who ever lived. Carter is always telling people that he is not Michael Jordan and does not want to be. He just tells them that he wants to be Vince Carter—and that is just fine with Carter's fans.

> "The next step will be his ability to take his team through the playoffs, like Bird, Magic, Isiah, Michael and now Kobe and Shaq."
>
> —Coach Doug Collins

In fact, Carter was named the Hometown Hero for May 2001 by the NBA for working to improve the community. Lots of people credit Carter's upbringing for him being one of the NBA's "good guys."

But if you ask Carter, some of the credit has to go to God. In fact, besides his nightly prayers, Carter makes it a point to speak to God at least two times every game night: once during the national anthem and once during the player introductions. Carter will close his eyes, attain a sense of quiet, and then just simply talk to God in his head. But Carter does not ask for help scoring 60 points or to be the player that

Vince Carter shakes hands with teammate Tracy McGrady just prior to a playoff game against the Knicks in New York's Madison Square Garden on April 23, 2000.

hits the game-winning shot at the buzzer. Instead, Carter prays that no one on the court gets injured and that he will play as hard as he can.

"I'm a Christian, so I pray at the games a lot, and that's what helps me relax. I know what God does for me," Carter said. "I'm not the most spiritual guy you know, but I do believe my ability comes from up above."[2]

In Carter's third season he led the Raptors to the playoffs once again. The team posted a 26–13 first-half record and even sent three players, including Carter, to the All-Star game.

While the team seemed to flourish under the veteran leadership of point guard Mark Jackson to help run the offense, the team felt he sometimes slowed Carter down. So just before the trading deadline the team shipped Jackson to the New York Knicks in exchange for younger and more athletic point guard Chris Childs. That trade sparked the young Raptors squad, which went on to win 19 of its next 27 games after the trade.

They were set to face the New York Knicks in the first round of the playoffs. It was the same Knicks team that eliminated the Raptors the previous season. But this time the Raptors knew what to expect.

The Knicks took the first game, but the Raptors bounced back and won the second by 20 points.

After the Raptors dropped the third game, there was a lot of talk in the newspapers and sports highlight shows that maybe Vince Carter was not tough enough to excel in playoff-style basketball. That talk angered Carter. He spent some time alone before game four thinking about all the things he had heard. Some Toronto fans even had the nerve to boo Carter as he was introduced before the must-win fourth game. Carter quickly turned the boos to cheers as he took control of the game right from the start. He dominated both ends of the court, scoring 32 points, passing for 4 assists and grabbing 7 rebounds.

> "I'm not the most spiritual guy you know, but I do believe my ability comes from up above."
>
> —Vince Carter

Now the Raptors would have to do the unthinkable. If they were to advance in the playoffs, they would have to win in New York's Madison Square Garden in the fifth and deciding game. The game was tight throughout. Both teams had plenty of opportunities to put the game away. That is when Carter put it all on the line and simply outworked and outhustled the Knicks during two key plays down the stretch. With only 1:25 left in the game and the Raptors up by a basket, Carter used his lightning speed to follow up on a missed basket, grab the rebound, and slam home the basket before anyone else on the court could even react. Then, with 42 seconds left in the game, he outhustled two Knicks near mid-court, grabbed the ball, and passed it to teammate Alvin Williams, who hit an open jump shot that put the Raptors up by six points with only 42 seconds left in the game. The Raptors won the game, 93–89.

NBA fans were salivating at the thought of the next matchup. High-flying Carter was going to go head-to-head with the Philadelphia 76ers and scoring machine Allen Iverson, who was the league's Most Valuable Player. It was a classic match-up, and both Carter and Iverson had games where they scored 50 points apiece. Scoring outbursts like that are astonishing in playoff basketball, where usually the emphasis is on defense and rebounding.

The Sixers were heavily favored to win the series—after all, they had recorded the best record in the Eastern Conference. But Carter and the pesky Raptors would not go away. The teams traded victories throughout and it came down to a deciding seventh game in Philadelphia. It would prove to be a special day for Vince Carter in many

Carter tries to keep Philadelphia's Allen Iverson from reaching the hoop.

ways. It began with a graduation ceremony at the University of North Carolina earlier that afternoon. In completing his degree, Carter fulfilled a promise he had made to his mother that he would go back and finish school. After the ceremony, Carter took a private plane to Philadelphia to meet up with Iverson and the Sixers in Game 7 that evening.

The Raptors kept the score incredibly close, and actually had a chance to win the game and take the series. With 54 seconds left in the game, Toronto's Dell Curry hit a three-pointer to pull the Raptors to within one, 88–87. At the other end, Iverson missed a jumper, but the Sixers got the rebound. They ran the clock down to 10 seconds before missing another jumper. This time, the Raptors got the rebound, but they failed to call timeout until there were just 3.6 seconds left. Philly still had a foul to give, which took the clock down to 2.0. Then, on the ensuing inbounds pass, Carter faked out Tyrone Hill to get open for the final shot. It was a twenty-three footer that flew just a little too long, rolling off the rim. The Sixers had won.

"All I can think about is that shot," Carter later said. "It's something you live for. Maybe next year."[3]

Still, it was a great experience for the young Raptors, and Carter had given the fans his all. He had once again had a great season with an awesome 27.6 points per game average. Carter had become one of the most dominating scorers in the league.

Unfortunately for the Raptors, the next two seasons would not be as fruitful. The team lost McGrady to the Orlando Magic, and Carter suffered a series of injuries. This did not allow Carter to get into a good groove on the basketball court, whenever he was healthy enough to be on it. Because of injuries he was limited to 60 games in the 2001–02 season and only 43 games for the 2002–03 campaign.

Carter found the injuries very frustrating. "Yeah, it does [ruin the season]," Carter said. "It's going to kill us every time."[4]

After struggling with injuries for much of two seasons, it seemed as if Carter was determined to make a statement in the season opener of 2003–04. In the game, Carter's Raptors met the two-time defending Eastern Conference champs, the New Jersey Nets—no easy match-up for Toronto. But Vince Carter came out strong and never let up, finishing with 39 points. Thirteen of these points came in crunch time, in the fourth quarter, lifting the Raptors to a 90–87 victory. Carter's 39 points were the highest point total in a season-opener in Raptors' history. Quite a performance from a player who had missed a combined total of 61 games over the previous two seasons.

"I'm excited to be back healthy and able to contribute to this team just because of what's gone on the past year and a half," Carter said. "We just wanted to be close in the fourth quarter and try to take over. . . . I just wanted to make things happen, whether it's putting the ball in the hole or finding someone open."[5]

Carter's clutch performance included hitting a fadeaway jumper with 50 seconds left to give Toronto an 84–83 lead. After New Jersey missed its next shot, Carter came back and hit another jumper to give the Raptors a three-point lead with 14 seconds left. The game marked the first season opener the Nets had lost in three years.

> "I just wanted to make things happen, whether it's putting the ball in the hole or finding someone open."
>
> —Vince Carter

"Since I have gotten here, I've said that the least of my worries is Vince [Carter]," Head Coach Kevin O'Neill said after the game. "The bottom line is that when he's healthy, he's pretty hard to deal with."[6]

"He [Carter] is back and with a vengeance," Raptors forward Jerome Williams added, "and we are going to keep riding [him]."[7]

Carter puts up a jump shot before the Nets' Jason Kidd can reach him during the 2003 season opener in Toronto on October 29, 2003.

Carter continued to thrive early on in the season. In a late-November game against the Hawks at Philips Arena in Atlanta, he poured in 43 points, leading Toronto to a 99–97 victory in overtime. Out of his 43 points, 33 came in the second half, which tied a Philips Arena record.

"We don't quit," Carter said of the game. "We just play until the end because you never know."[8]

After leading by as many as 16 points in the first half, Atlanta held a 70–62 lead at the end of the third quarter. But Carter led a comeback by scoring 16 points in the fourth. He single-handedly forced overtime with a spectacular spin move in the lane to shake loose Hawks guard Dion Glover. He then flipped the ball in off the glass while being fouled by center Theo Ratliff. Carter sank the free throw to complete the three-point play with 13 seconds left to tie the game.

"I was just trying to make the play," Carter later said. "We needed two points and I was trying to get fouled."[9]

In overtime, Carter drilled an 18-footer to give the Raptors a one-point lead with 4.3 seconds left. Then, on the other end of the floor, he came up with a huge defensive play, blocking Jason Terry's shot with just one second left on the clock.

"For him to make the plays he did down the stretch, including the defensive block at the end, that's what he gets paid max money for," said Raptors Head Coach Kevin O'Neill. "And that's what he did. He played like a max player."[10]

"You just saw another Vince Carter performance at Philips Arena," Hawks coach Terry Stotts said after the game. "I think his last 10 or 12 points were tough shots that were contested. He just carried them [the Raptors]."[11]

> "We don't quit. We just play until the end because you never know."
> —Vince Carter

NBA fans took notice. In late January, the results of the fan balloting for the 2004 All-Star Game were announced. Carter led the league in votes received with 2,127,183. It would be Carter's fifth all-star selection and the fourth time in his young career that he led all vote-getters. This tied him with Hall of Famer "Dr. J," Julius Erving for second place all-time in NBA history. (Michael Jordan is first, having led the league in total votes nine times.)

A healthy Carter promises to be one of the most explosive and exciting players in the NBA for many years to come. And even though some aches and pains have slowed him down a bit on the hardwood, there is very little that can slow Carter down off the court.

Vince Carter is one of those rare people who just loves getting involved in causes and helping those who are not as fortunate as he is. One of the ways that he helps those in need is by hosting a basketball tournament in his hometown of Daytona Beach every summer. He calls it the Vince Carter Summertime Jam. Carter holds a similar event in Toronto. In 2001, the events raised more than $400,000 for the Ronald McDonald House and the Boys and Girls Clubs. And that is just the beginning.

Carter regularly delivers Christmas toys and presents to children associated with the Children's Home Society. Carter does so much for the group that it named him the Child Advocate of the Year. Carter's mother is always bragging to the media, not about her son's basketball skills, but about how much he loves children. Carter established his own foundation to help numerous children's charities. He calls it Embassy of Hope.

Carter also has been named a Goodwill Ambassador by the Big Brothers/Big Sisters of America. His generosity was really highlighted when he donated $2.5 million to his old school, Mainland

Carter attempts to block the shot of Dion Glover of the Atlanta Hawks.

High, when he heard it was trying to raise money for a new gymnasium.

"This is something that's in my heart," Carter said. "I love Mainland. This is my way of saying thank you. It's not all about having it all and keeping it for yourself. Using what I have to better others and brighten their day, that's a great feeling."[12]

Vince Carter's fans would agree that it is also a great feeling hearing about all the good things Carter does as well as watching his unmatched skills on the basketball court.

CHAPTER NOTES

Chapter I. Greatest Game

1. Tom Maloney, "Stopping the Vinsanity," *The Sporting News*, January 28, 2002, p. 6.
2. Ibid.
3. Ibid.
4. Associated Press, "Carter inVINCEable over Suns," February 27, 2000.
5. Ibid.
6. Ibid.

Chapter 2. Growing Up

1. "Growing Up," *Flight VC: Vince Carter 15*, n.d., <http://www.flightvc.com.go.to/> (August 26, 2003).
2. Ibid.
3. "Making A Name," *Flight VC: Vince Carter 15*, n.d., <http://www.flightvc.com.go.to/> (March 2, 2004).
4. Ibid.
5. "Vince's Love for Music," *Flight VC: Vince Carter 15*, n.d., <http://www.flightvc.com.go.to/> (August 26, 2003).
6. Ibid.
7. Ibid.
8. "Making A Name," *Flight VC: Vince Carter 15*.
9. Ibid.

Chapter 3. The Big Recruit

1. "Making a Name," *Flight VC: Vince Carter 15*, n.d., <http://www.flightvc.com.go.to/> (August 26, 2003).
2. Ibid.
3. "Being Recruited by Top Colleges," *Flight VC: Vince Carter 15*, n.d., <http://www.flightvc.com.go.to/> (August 26, 2003).
4. Ibid.
5. Ibid.
6. "Becoming a Tar Heel," *Flight VC: Vince Carter 15*, n.d., <http://www.flightvc.com.go.to/> (August 26, 2003).

Chapter 4. Tar Heel Superstar

1. "Becoming a Tar Heel," *Flight VC: Vince Carter 15*, n.d., <http://www.flightvc.com.go.to/> (August 26, 2003).
2. Ibid.
3. Ibid.
4. "Sophomore Year at UNC," *Flight VC: Vince Carter 15*, n.d., <http://www.flightvc.com.go.to/> (August 26, 2003).
5. "Junior Year at UNC," *Flight VC: Vince Carter 15*, n.d., <http://www.flightvc.com.go.to/> (August 26, 2003).

Chapter 5. The NBA

1. "Junior Year at UNC," *Flight VC: Vince Carter 15*, n.d., <http://www.flightvc.com.go.to/> (August 26, 2003).
2. Ron Kroichick, "He's Catching Up," *The Sporting News*, March 5, 2001, p. 12.
3. Kevin Chappell, "Is Vince Carter the Next Michael Jordan?" *Ebony* Magazine, April 2000, p. 32.

4. Kroichick.

5. Chappell.

6. Ibid.

7. Ibid.

8. Ibid.

Chapter 6. A Genuine Good Guy

1. Tom Maloney, "I'm Not Mike!" *The Sporting News*, January 28, 2002, p. 28.

2. Darryl Howerton, "A Higher Power," *NBA.com*, 2002, <http://www.nba.com/publications/is_carter_jan.html> (August 27, 2003).

3. Associated Press, "Survival Skills," *SportsIllustrated. CNN.com*, May 21, 2001, <http://sportsillustrated.cnn.com/basketball/nba/2001/playoffs/news/2001/05/20/raptors_sixers_ap/> (March 2, 2004).

4. "Vince Carter Interview," *Inside Hoops.com*, March 25, 2003, <http://www.insidehoops.com/vince-carter-interview-032503.html> (August 27, 2003).

5. *NBA.com*, October 29, 2003, <http://www.nba.com/raptors/news/instant_replay_031029.html> (January 30, 2004).

6. Ibid.

7. Ibid.

8. "Toronto 99, Atlanta 97 (ot)," *SportsIllustrated. CNN.com*, November 26, 2003, <http://sportsillustrated.cnn.com/basketball/nba/recaps/2003/11/26/16309_recap.html> (January 30, 2004).

9. Ibid.

10. Ibid.

11. Ibid.

12. Associated Press, "Carter Donates $2.5 Million to High School," September 16, 2002.

CAREER STATISTICS

COLLEGE

SEASON	TEAM	GP	FG%	REB	PTS	AVG
1995–1996	North Carolina	31	.492	119	232	7.5
1996–1997	North Carolina	34	.525	152	443	13.0
1997–1998	North Carolina	38	.591	195	592	15.6
TOTALS		103	.547	466	1,267	12.3

GP—Games Played REB—Rebounds
FG%—Field Goal PTS—Points
Percentage AVG—Average

NBA

SEASON	TEAM	GP	FG%	REB	AST	STL	BLK	PTS	AVG
1998–1999	Toronto	50	.450	283	149	55	77	913	18.3
1999–2000	Toronto	82	.465	476	322	110	92	2,107	25.7
2000–2001	Toronto	75	.460	416	291	114	82	2,070	27.6
2001–2002	Toronto	60	.428	313	239	94	43	1,484	24.7
2002–2003	Toronto	43	.467	188	143	48	41	884	20.6
2003–2004	Toronto	73	.417	349	348	88	65	1,645	22.5
TOTALS		383	.447	2,025	1,492	509	400	9,103	23.8

GP—Games Played REB—Rebounds BLK—Blocks
FG%—Field Goal AST—Assists PTS—Points
Percentage STL—Steals AVG—Average

WHERE
TO WRITE

Mr. Vince Carter
c/o Toronto Raptors
40 Bay Street, Suite 400
Toronto, Ontario 5MJ 2

INTERNET ADDRESSES

Vince Carter Official Website

http://www.vincecarter15.com/

Vince Carter Player File

http://www.nba.com/playerfile/vince_carter/index.
html

Toronto Raptors Homepage

http://www.nba.com/raptors

INDEX